This book is dedicated to Mrs. Johnson.

Copyright © 2025 Jennifer Jones
All copyright laws and rights reserved.
Published in the U.S.A.
For more information, email info@ninjalifehacks.tv
Paperback ISBN: 978-1-63731-922-2
Hardcover ISBN: 978-1-63731-924-6
eBook ISBN: 978-1-63731-923-9

Find the Instruments on Strike lesson plans at ninjalifehacks.tv

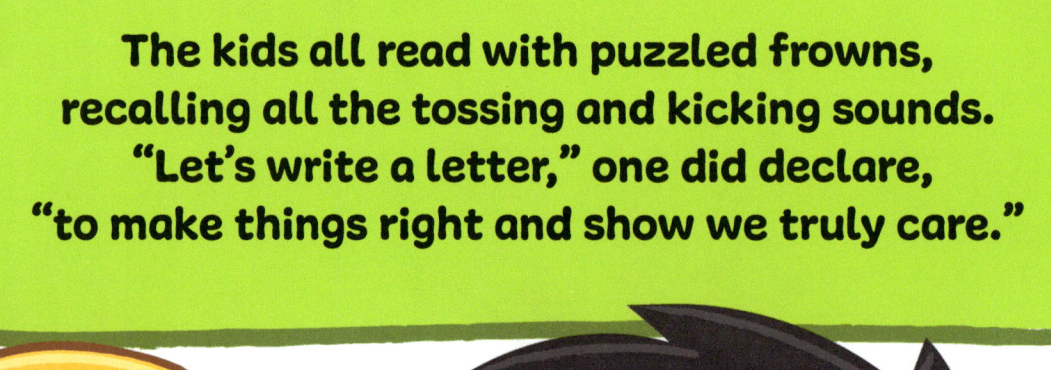

The kids all read with puzzled frowns,
recalling all the tossing and kicking sounds.
"Let's write a letter," one did declare,
"to make things right and show we truly care."

Dear Instruments, please forgive us

for all the times we caused a fuss.

We'll be gentle. We do swear.

Come back. We'll show you we care.

www.ingramcontent.com/pod-product-compliance
Lightning Source LLC
Chambersburg PA
CBHW042148200426
43209CB00066B/1827